STEPHEN MARCHE

On Writing *and* Failure

Or, On the Peculiar Perseverance

Required to Endure the Life of a Writer

BIBLIOASIS

Windsor, Ontario

FIRST EDITION
10 9 8 7 6 5 4 3

Library and Archives Canada Cataloguing in Publication

Title: On writing and failure, or, on the peculiar perseverance required to
endure the life of a writer / Stephen Marche.
Other titles: On the peculiar perseverance required to endure the life of a
writer
Names: Marche, Stephen, author.
Series: Field notes (Biblioasis) ; #6.
Description: Series statement: Field notes ; 6
Identifiers: Canadiana (print) 20220476047 | Canadiana (ebook) 20220476152
| ISBN 9781771965163 (softcover) | ISBN 9781771965170 (EPUB)
Subjects: LCSH: Marche, Stephen. | LCSH: Authorship.
Classification: LCC PS8626.A723 Z46 2023 | DDC C813/.6—dc23

Edited by Daniel Wells
Copyedited by Chandra Wohleber
Typeset by Vanessa Stauffer
Series designed by Ingrid Paulson

Published with the generous assistance of the Canada Council for the Arts,
which last year invested $153 million to bring the arts to Canadians throughout
the country, and the financial support of the Government of Canada. Biblioasis
also acknowledges the support of the Ontario Arts Council (OAC), an agency of
the Government of Ontario, which last year funded 1,709 individual artists
and 1,078 organizations in 204 communities across Ontario, for a total of
$52.1 million, and the contribution of the Government of Ontario through the
Ontario Book Publishing Tax Credit and Ontario Creates.

PRINTED AND BOUND IN CANADA

Talent is insignificant. I know a lot of talented ruins. Beyond talent lie all the usual words: discipline, love, luck, but, most of all, endurance.

—James Baldwin

Any life when viewed from the inside is simply a series of defeats.

—George Orwell

"IS IT EVER easier?" a kid writer asked me recently. "Do you ever grow a thicker skin?" She was suffering, poor thing, after a gorgeous essay about the death of her mother had been rejected by every outlet that could publish it. I had no answer, so I told her a story. Just before the outbreak of COVID, Nathan Englander, the short story writer and novelist, had moved into my neighbourhood in Toronto, and we would sometimes sit around my back-yard firepit, drinking and complaining. "Is it ever easier?" I asked him one night. "Do you ever grow a thicker skin?" At the time, some magazine editor had fucked me over, I forget about what. Englander had no answer, so he told me a story. He had been lunching with Philip Roth once. "Is it ever easier?" he asked Roth. "Do you ever grow a thicker skin?" Englander was then about to release a new novel, always a toxically anxious period. Roth didn't need a story. He had an answer. "Your skin just grows thinner and thinner," Roth told him. "In the end, they can hold you up to the light and see right through you."

* * *

FAILURE IS THE body of a writer's life. Success is only ever an attire. A paradox defines this business: The public only sees writers in their victories but their real lives are

7

mostly in defeat. I suppose that's why, in the rare moments of triumph, writers always look so out of place—posing on the Books page in their half-considered outfits with their last-minute hair, desperately upping their most positive reviews on Instagram, or, at the strange ceremonies of writing prizes, like the Oscars for lumpy people, grinning like recently released prisoners readjusting themselves to society.

Failure is big right now—a subject of commencement speeches and business conferences like FailCon, at which triumphant entrepreneurs detail all their ideas that went bust. But businessmen are only amateurs at failure, just getting used to the notion. Writers are the real professionals. Three hundred thousand books are published every year in the United States alone. A few hundred, at most, could be called financial or creative successes. The majority of books by successful writers are failures. The majority of writers are failures. And then there are the would-be writers, those who have failed to be writers in the first place, a category which, if you believe what people tell you at parties, constitutes the bulk of the species.

For every Shakespeare who retired to the country and to permanent fame, there are a thousand who took hard breaks and vanished: George Chapman, the first translator of Homer, begging in the streets because his patrons kept dying on him; Thomas Dekker, whose hair went white in debtors' prison; and my personal favourite, the playwright John Webster, whose birth and death dates in the *Dictionary of Literary Biography* are question marks, symbolic hooks into oblivion. He wrote *The Duchess of Malfi* and nobody knows where he came from or where he ended up.

I am writing this essay because I would like somebody to be halfway honest about what it takes to live as a writer, in air clear from the fumes of pompous incense. The first job of a writer is to write. The second job is to persevere. If you want to write, or if you want to know what it's like to write, you're going to have to walk away from the paths of glory into the dark wilderness. Because that's where it is.

* * *

THE DOMINANT NARRATIVE, at the moment, is that failure leads to success. The internet loves this arc: low then high; first perseverance, then making it; all struggle redeemed; the more struggle the more redemption. It's pure bullshit, but not for the reason most people think.

I've been lucky enough to know some of the most successful writers of my generation, men and women who have earned hundreds of millions of dollars, who have won all the prizes, who have received all the accolades, who have achieved fame insofar as writerly fame exists. The triumphs don't seem to make much difference. A hundred million dollars is worth having, to be sure, but it doesn't protect you from the sense that you've been misunderstood, that the world doesn't recognize who you are. It doesn't. I know if you're a kid writer you must think I'm either lying or they're crazy. All I can tell you is that I'm not lying.

From my own experience, I would even go so far as to say that the more celebrated the writer, the more fraught the struggle. In 2010, Jonathan Franzen talked to Terry Gross about what turned out to be his massive bestseller *Freedom*. "I thought I'd written a book that I might, worst case, have to hand-sell," he said. "I figured if I could get two hundred people to listen to a half-hour reading, they might want to read the book, and then it would spread by word of mouth." This was after he had sold 1.6 million copies of *The Corrections* and made an appearance on the cover of *Time*.

A friend of mine, a fellow novelist, ran into Margaret Atwood at a party once, and, as a way of introducing himself, mentioned an op-ed he'd written in the *New York Times* on the subject of Orhan Pamuk, a writer they both admired. Automatically, defensively, she snapped back, "I've written for the *Times*, too." My novelist friend ate out on this story because, to him, and to me, and everyone we knew, she was Margaret Atwood and we were a bunch of chancers. Only after we aged, and accumulated a few accidental successes, did we understand that Atwood is a chancer. She's a chancer even though she's on a stamp. Everybody who writes is a chancer.

The psychology of failure and success can work the other way, too. I knew a professor once who published a single letter in the *Times Literary Supplement*. He constantly brought it up. He had it framed, hung on his wall. On the basis of that letter he considered himself a major intellectual, a part of "the larger conversation." And who's to say he's wrong? Maybe the works of Margaret Atwood and Jonathan Franzen will slowly disappear and later scholars will discover and celebrate "The *TLS* letter."

* * *

NO AMOUNT OF success is a protection from the spectre of obscurity. There's no amulet against oblivion. Ever hear

of Fitz-Greene Halleck? "No name in the American poet-
ical world is more firmly established than that of
Fitz-Greene Halleck," Edgar Allan Poe wrote in 1843.
There's a statue of the man in Central Park. Now nobody
knows him but the few Brooklyn hipsters who have
named July 8 Fitz-Greene Halleck Day. They go and read
his poetry at the statue. They're not celebrating him so
much as they're celebrating literary obscurity or, in the
end, their own affectation for literary obscurity. I first
read Fitz-Greene Halleck in Ezra Pound's poetry anthol-
ogy *Confucius to Cummings*. (From which he excluded
Pope. Is there a circle of success into which even Alexander Pope doesn't fall?) Does it matter that Fitz-Greene
Halleck's poetry is fantastic—deft and witty and roiling
with suppressed longings? It only slightly matters. There
are fashions in eternity as in all things.

* * *

RIGHT NOW, THE power of failure happens to be swelling,
accelerating. The condition of failure is a constant in
writerly life but the current generation of writers lives
with more failure than the previous generation, and the
next generation will live with more failure than the current generation.

I have only ever made a living inside crumbling
institutions—I know no one who feels differently. I began
teaching humanities just as jobs in the humanities vanished and writing novels as television replaced novels.
Then I started in journalism, just as it was imploding.
Sometimes I wondered if it was me, that my curse fell
upon an industry as I entered it, tumbling its pillars. But

paranoia is a brand of self-importance I am old enough to recognize.

The writing of our time is in constant, unrelenting transition. Whole schemes of meaning dissolve or rot or flame out, leaving only ashes and uncertain memories of a bright flash. For eight years, I was a monthly columnist for *Esquire* magazine. Column-writing was a practice, well-developed by tradition and the marketplace: Editors would send me a "zeitgeist list," containing all the new major cultural releases three months in advance. I would scan the previews, read books, see films. My thousand words often took a week to compose; skilled and dedicated editors would grind them through five or six edits. I was paid enough to support myself on one column a month. That whole system ended five years ago, but it already seems a relic from some half-mythic era, like the antebellum South or San Francisco during the Summer of Love.

The "hot takes" era drifted in somewhere in the middle of my life as a columnist. I posted as often as three or four times a week. I remember once, I started cooking dinner, some VIP died, my editor called me for an obit, I put my laptop on the counter, I wrote the piece before the meal was cooked, it was published by the time we finished eating. The hot takes era is mostly dead now. No one mourns it.

Two sensations have defined my writerly life: Scanning the horizon constantly for threat or prey, and jumping from ice floe to ice floe on a river in spring flood. Every few years there's some new great hope—right now it's Substack. Substack will die or peter out just like the rest.

I have seen the best minds of my generation devote their souls to business plans—even the smallest up-and-comer has a social media marketing strategy; the biggest of the big start streaming services. Everywhere, in ersatz dive bars and in university cafés and imitation osterias, poets and drummers and video artists discuss the decline of digital ad revenues and online pledge systems and merch. I have not met a single artist, in any field, who is not, if you get right to the bottom of their lives, pursuing the crudest form of personal material security out of necessity. The principal question of the life of the mind has become how to make a living at the life of the mind. It is unfathomably anxiety-making and boring.

And it's not like these transitions take place over the course of a lifetime. All this shit happened in the past ten years. Each transition requires starting over, reevaluating, submitting, and above all, failing. The younger the writer, the more chaotic their future. Just to survive, kid writers today will have to live through multiple revisions of who they are and what they do. The modes they're learning, the writerly identities they hunger to inhabit, won't exist or won't be recognizable during most of their writing lives.

* * *

PART OF THE problem, for writers of my generation any-way, is that we're living in an aftermath. The peace and prosperity of the postwar era gave birth to an array of lit-erary institutions that have been in managed decline ever since. Novelists were legitimate celebrities. New York was full of middle-class playwrights who wrote small excellent plays and somehow survived. Professorships were avail-able; job applications were not hunger games. Magazines and newspapers had vast profit margins and masses of pages to fill. And all this power, the money and the institutions, provided the writers of that generation with a sense of cosmic self-importance no one can rival today.

The Boomers' writing lives were exceptions. We are returning to the historical standard. A golden age has given way to an age of chaos. One mode of writing—print—is dying and another mode of writing—digital—is being born. Writing has seen such transition before. In the eighteenth century in England, a whole generation of writers found themselves stuck between patronage and professionalism. Some writers jumped over the crack. Others fell through. Just like now. That's why the career of a writer like Samuel Johnson is more relevant to our moment than the career of any Boomer writer.

At thirty, Samuel Johnson was broke as fuck. He was worse than broke. He had a wife, much older than himself, who needed more money than he could earn. For her health, Tetty couldn't live in London. For his work, Johnson couldn't live anywhere else. Any money he made he sent away. A friend who knew him at the time claimed that Johnson "subsisted himself for a considerable space of time upon the scanty pittance of fourpence halfpenny a day." The hackwork was brutal. He took every assignment. The House of Commons, in 1738, banned reports of parliamentary debates, so for the *Gentleman's Magazine* Johnson devised the scheme of turning the debates into fiction, using the setting of Lilliput from Jonathan Swift's *Gulliver's Travels*. (They didn't even try to hide the names. Walpole became Walelop. Pitt became Ptit.) Johnson did the shit work, like judging poetry prizes. He classed the magazine up a bit by writing Latin verses. He translated *The History of the Council of Trent*, told hooker life stories, spread gossip. Anything that could be printed that there might be the slightest market for he sold or tried to sell. It was never enough. It never is.

Writers don't often talk about their rejections, even among one another. Sometimes, though, they use the lives of others to describe their pain. Johnson used Richard Savage as his failure double. Savage was in a worse state than Johnson, because money poured through him. After scarlet cloaks with gold lace became the fashion, Johnson ran into Savage "with one of these cloaks upon his back, while, at the same time, his naked toes were peeping through his shoes." Besides being vain and a spendthrift, Savage was also a prick. You couldn't tell him anything in confidence because he betrayed confidences the moment you had an argument. He was quick to fight and "he considered himself as discharged by the first quarrel from all ties of honour or gratitude." He made friends easily. He lost friends easily.

Savage and Johnson shared the gutter, the best friendship incubator. Sometimes they did not have even enough money for the flophouses, so they would walk the streets all night. Savage knew the spots to lie down "with his associates in poverty, among the ashes of a glass-house." One night, they circled St. James's Square over and over. "They were not at all depressed by their situation," Joshua Reynolds remembered Johnson telling him, "but in high spirits and brimful of patriotism, traversed the square for several hours, inveighed against the minister, and 'resolved they would *stand by their country*.'" Like every loser, Savage had his little sob story. He told everyone, and he probably believed, that he was the illegitimate son of Anne Mason, the Countess of Macclesfield. The Countess of Macclesfield failed to approve this assessment. Savage's attempts to wrangle acknowledgement, and money, out of his supposed mother failed. He regarded himself as an aristocratic victim of maternal contempt, a fine position for a confirmed moocher. He overwhelmed himself, and tried to overwhelm others, with his particular brand of self-pity.

Johnson swallowed the whole bit about the aristocratic mother. He bought Savage's version of everything. After Savage murdered a man in an argument about a seat by the fire in a coffee house, he survived a death sentence through the intercession of the Countess of Hertford. "His merit and his calamities happened to reach the ear of the Countess of Hertford, who engaged in his support with all the tenderness that is excited by pity, and all the zeal which is kindled by generosity," Johnson wrote in his *Life of Savage*, "and demanding an audience of the Queen, laid before her the whole series of his mother's cruelty, exposed the improbability of an accusation by which he was charged with an intent to commit a murder that could produce no advantage, and soon convinced her how little his former conduct could deserve to be mentioned as a reason for extraordinary severity." Savage was at least half-criminal. He was a criminal who needs the eyeball witness. There are writers who become criminals so that there will be an eyeball witness.

Savage was just another fucked-up writer. There are plenty of those. His friends tried to take care of him. Alexander Pope set up a subscription to provide him with an annual pension on the condition that he keep himself out in Wales. That's not how it works with the fuck-ups. He kept going into Bristol with his friends' money. He died in debtor's prison there in 1743.

An Account of the Life of Mr. Richard Savage, probably the best thing Johnson ever wrote, ends with a plea for mercy. "For his life, or for his writings, none who candidly consider his fortune will think an apology either necessary or difficult," Johnson writes. "Those are no proper judges of his conduct who have slumbered away their time on the down of plenty, nor will a wise man presume to say 'Had I been in Savage's condition, I should have lived, or written, better than Savage.'" Samuel Johnson was rarely merciful in his judgments, even to his friends. Johnson's plea for mercy for Savage was, obviously, also a plea for mercy for himself. "On a bulk, in a cellar, or in a glass-house among thieves and beggars, was to be found the author of *The Wanderer*, the man of exalted sentiments, extensive views, and curious observations, the man whose remarks on life might have assisted the statesman, whose ideas of virtue might have enlightened the moralist, whose eloquence might have influenced senates, and whose delicacy might have polished courts." "Might have" is the cry of every artist who has to hustle, who has to reconcile the dreams of art with the realities of shifting marketplaces. Writers want to be judged by what they could have written. The world insists on judging them by the reception of what they have written. Careers are circumstances. Others treat them as the unfolding of an inner truth.

Johnson and Savage were countrymen: The nation of writers is a nation of three-legged dogs. Every seed is a seed that's fallen on hard ground.

* * *

ENGLISH HAS PROVIDED a precise term of art to describe the writerly condition: Submission. Writers live in a state of submission. Submission means rejection. Rejection is the condition of the practice of submission, which is the practice of writing.

Again, we happen to inhabit a period of radical turbulence. Digital culture expands the possibility of rejection exponentially. It seems incredible but I've known writers who used to submit, literally, the manuscript of a work. It might loiter for six months in some publishers' office before being returned by way of a self-addressed stamped envelope. Under the conditions of print, a dozen failures a year were difficult to accumulate. Today, if you work at it, you can fail a dozen times before lunch.

I kept a scrupulous account of my rejections until I reached the two thousand mark. That was in my late twenties. Because I work in a range of genres, with pitching an idea as easy as sending an email, I have had the opportunity to be rejected at a rate impossible to earlier writers. Last week, I was rejected seven times. I had to go back and check. I don't notice rejection much anymore.

Occasionally, I will meet with a kid writer who has confused me with somebody to be envied. They want to know what it's like to write professionally. My good news is the same as my bad news. Rejection never ends. Success is no cure. Success only alters to whom, or what, you may submit. Rejection is the river in which we swim. If you are sending short stories to literary journals, you are engaged in the same activity as Ian McEwan. The difference is one of scale, not of kind or of quality. It is hard to explain to kid writers. The problem is probably not that they're being rejected too much. The problem is that they're not being rejected enough. They tell you to develop calluses. It's not enough. You have to relish the rejection. Rejection is the evidence of your hustle. Rejection is the sign that you are throwing yourself against the door.

All creative careers demand persistence because all creative careers require luck. Persistence is the siege you lay on fortune. In one sense, the subject of this book applies to many different creative fields. In 2015, at a sxsw session, casting directors from Fox, Paramount, and Disney estimated that the talent of any actor counted for about 7 percent of the reason they were cast in any given role. Age and ethnicity and "box office value in China" all mattered more. Success as an actor is only incidentally related to talent or effort. Painters and sculptors and designers and dancers and musicians all create under the same capriciousness of fortune. Even so, the life of a writer demands a peculiar persistence. Writers make meaning. They trade, equally, in illusion and disillusion. To live in the quaking of meaning is to shudder from your feet up.

There are writers who write and there are writers who want to be writers. (There is a third group who simply have something to write and go out and write it. They are blessed. I have nothing to offer them.) If you are writing because you want to be a writer, I would very much like to dissuade you from that ambition. Trying to find fulfillment through writing is like trying to fly by jumping off a cliff. "Vanity of vanities, all is vanity," says the preacher in Ecclesiastes. "My son, be admonished: of making many books there is no end, and much study is a weariness of flesh." Ecclesiastes may be the oldest essay ever written;

its point is the pointlessness of essays. We always knew this was vanity. We kept going anyway.

* * *

PERSEVERANCE IS THE true subject of all literary biography. The truth of perseverance always remains hidden. Again, there's a paradox: Any subject of a literary biography has succeeded to the point of being considered a fit subject for a literary biography. The pain and the conflict grow misted in the comforting glow of the conclusion the existence of the book itself proves, that it all worked out in the end and the talent achieved recognition. That's not true nearly all of the time.

There is, supposedly, the Life and there is the Work, and all manner of philosophical surgeons separate them or conjoin them. How does the Life shape the Work? Can a Bad Life lead to Great Work? Is the Work what matters, or is it the Life? These questions assume a faith in literary transcendence. But the business of using Life to make Work is not transcendent. It is struggle. It is grind. Writing may be a cosmic howl, the pursuit of humanity's proper place in the universe and a glorious reckoning with the limits of meaning itself, but it's also a job. For a lucky few, the job is like running a failing haberdashery. For the majority it's more like trying to sell T-shirts out of the trunks of their cars.

Neither talent nor intelligence nor clarity of purpose seem to make much difference. George Orwell finished *Animal Farm* in 1943, a short, topical allegory that needed to be published quickly to reflect the realities of Stalinist repression then under way. No big publishing house would touch it. "More public-spirited pigs," was T. S. Eliot's note in his rejection letter, though he admitted, "We have no conviction (and I am sure none of the other directors would have) that this is the right point of view from which to criticize the political situation at the present time." Eliot was nodding to the obvious. During the Second World War, it was simply not possible to publish a critique of Russia, a major Western ally. Even Republicans were pro-Stalin in 1943. *Animal Farm*'s intended effect never had the slightest chance of landing. By the time the book found its way into print, in 1945, the political situation had altered; it became one of the major texts of anti-Communist hysteria. Which was not what it was supposed to be at all.

So you can say what you like about Orwell and his Work and his Life and his Times, but his experience of his Times was creating a small masterpiece he couldn't make anyone publish, then living long enough to see it misunderstood. If it was like that for Orwell, why would it be any different for you?

* * *

NO MATTER THE times, the times are against writers. In the early eleventh century, in Persia, Abolqasem Ferdowsi composed the Shahnameh, a grand epic over fifty thousand lines long, describing history from the origins of the world to the Arab conquest of the seventh century. The whole point of his vast undertaking was to promote the independent Islamic Persian Samanids, but then the Ghaznavid Turks conquered the Persian Samanids, and though Ferdowsi tried to revise his masterpiece to please the new bosses, he couldn't revise enough. He finished fifty thousand lines of some of the greatest poetry ever composed with a big whinge: "My star was a laggard one. Nobles and great men wrote down what I had written without paying me: I watched them from a distance, as if I were a hired servant of theirs. I had nothing from them but their congratulations; my gall bladder was ready to burst with their congratulations! Their purses of hoarded coins remained closed, and my bright heart grew weary at their stinginess." The whole national history, from the Demon-King Zahhak through the seven trials of Rostam to the reign of Yazdegerd, ends with the writer complaining that nobody understands him and he's broke.

Every literary essay takes the form of complaint.

* * *

I DON'T WANT to hear any whining. I really don't. To become a successful plumber requires talent, dedication, and luck. To become excellent as a waiter, as a florist, as an upholsterer, requires sacrifice. I guess because writers so often emerge out of academic institutions, it takes them a while to recognize how tough it is to make a living. You think it should be easy to sell your feelings? You want to be congratulated for it? You want them to throw you a big party?

The internet loves to tell stories about famous writers facing adversity. Jack London kept his letters of rejection impaled on a spindle, and eventually the pile rose to four feet, around six hundred rejections. Marcel Proust and Beatrix Potter had to self-publish. It took Agatha Christie five years to find her way into print. There are a thousand examples—*Twilight* was rejected fourteen times, *The Diary of Anne Frank* fifteen times, *A Wrinkle in Time* twenty-six, *Gone with the Wind* thirty-eight, and so on. These stories are supposed to be inspiring or a testament to the idiocy of the literary gatekeepers or something. What I find strange is that anyone finds it strange that there's so much rejection. The average telemarketer has to make eighteen calls before finding someone willing to talk with him or her. And that's for shit people might need, like a vacuum cleaner or a new smartphone. Nobody needs a manuscript.

* * *

Don't tell me about failures on the way to success. Don't tell me about how it's all going to work out. Don't show me J. K. Rowling scribbling her children's book on the train with draft paper because she couldn't afford notebooks. Those stories are about as useful as lottery ads are to retirement planning. If you want inspiration, show me Johnson passed out on the glass-house floor, show me Melville scribbling *Billy Budd* on breaks from the customs house, Keats listening to the fountain by the Spanish Steps, Anna Akhmatova begging her friends to memorize her lines because she was too afraid to write them down. Those are legitimate goals. Those are real ambitions.

* * *

NO WHINING. EVERY serious publisher turned down Nabokov's *Lolita*, which you could argue (I would) is the finest short novel of the twentieth century. The only guy who would publish it was an indifferent Parisian pornographer who literally selected titles on the basis that they had been banned. Maurice Girodias told an interviewer from *Playboy* that he was willing to accept the title of pornographer "with joy and pride," and that the aim of his list was "to be indiscriminate, to bring out good books as well as bad ones: the only standard was the ostracism to which they would have been subjected." Nabokov's agent reported that Girodias's enthusiasm for *Lolita* had much less to do with the book's supple psychological interplay of horror and sympathy, or the lucid fascination of the sentences raised to maximum expressivity, or the allegory of the encounter between Europe and America, and more to do with outright support for pedophilia: "He finds the book not only admirable from the literary point of view, but he thinks that it might lead to a change in social attitudes toward the kind of love described in *Lolita*, provided of course, that it has this authenticity, this burning and irrepressible ardor." The publisher believed that Nabokov was a self-justifying pedophile. His masterpiece was published on that basis. In later life, Nabokov squirmed at a trick-or-treater, eight years old, who came to his door costumed as Lolita asking for Halloween candy.

* * *

NO WHINING. JANE Austen never lived to see her name on any of her books. They were "By A Lady." Every Jane Austen novel, with the exception of *Pride and Prejudice*, had to be published on commission, with the expenses of publication paid for by the author, the publisher taking a fee for services.

* * *

NO WHINING. THE next time you're rejected from some grant or some job, remember James Joyce in 1912. He had just turned thirty. He was living with his wife and a couple of kids in Italy, in self-imposed exile. His landlord was threatening to evict him for rent arrears. In desperation, he applied for a job teaching English at a local technical college, the Instituto Tecnico di Como, but he didn't have the necessary qualifications and sat an examination in Padua for a teaching diploma—three days of written work, followed by an oral exam. Literary history presents us with the scene of James Joyce, who had, by that point, already written *Dubliners* and most of *A Portrait of the Artist as a Young Man*, attempting to prove to administrators at an Italian technical college that he knew how English worked.

In support of his job application, he lectured at the Universita del Popolo on *Robinson Crusoe*. That talk may be the single greatest lecture on an individual novel ever given. Its final lines are as loaded with treasure as anything in his novels: "Saint John the Evangelist saw on the island of Patmos the apocalyptic collapse of the universe and the raising up of the walls of the eternal city splendid with beryl and emerald, onyx and jasper, sapphires and rubies. Crusoe saw but one marvel in all the fertile creation that surrounded him, a naked footprint in the virgin sand: and who knows if the latter does not matter more than the former?" He wrote *that* and it didn't matter. The invigilators in Padua denied him the diploma because they didn't recognize his Irish degree.

That's James Joyce we're talking about here. He couldn't get a job as a low-level lecturer at a technical college. Joyce's biography is one failure after another, a combination of bad luck and total ineffectiveness. He was not dishonest or weak or lacking in cunning. It's just that things never seemed to work out. He was the kind of guy who couldn't win for losing. He ended up teaching English as a second language as a private tutor, the equivalent of putting up flyers on the street offering guitar lessons.

Anyone with the desire to make art with words should be aware that James Joyce—James fucking Joyce—couldn't make a living at it. Deserving has nothing to do with it.

* * *

SOMETIMES DESERVING MAKES it harder. A particularly cruel species of irony drove the working life of Herman Melville. His first book was *Typee: A Peep at Polynesian Life*, pure crap and a significant bestseller. His final book was *Billy Budd*, an extreme masterpiece he couldn't even manage to self-publish. His fate was like the sick joke of some cruel god. The better he wrote, the more he failed.

"Though I wrote the Gospels in this century, I should die in the gutter," he complained to his mentor Nathaniel Hawthorne. As the light of his abilities rose, the darkness of his career set on. *Moby-Dick* sold 1,500 copies the first month, 2,300 over the next year and a half. Melville's lifetime earnings for the Great American Novel came to 1,260 bucks. For his next book—a seriously wonderful novel, *Pierre, or The Ambiguities*—part of the advance had to go to royalties already earned, and he took a flat twenty cents a copy on sales. Each deal, from then on, was smaller than the last. With *Battle-Pieces*, his collection of poems about the Civil War, he lost 400 dollars, after only 486 of the 1,260 sold.

Melville made of his fate what he could. After *Battle-Pieces*, he took a government job as a customs inspector. At times, he dreamed himself a degraded visionary, a glorious hidden genius, and at other times he found himself a wife-beating drunken clerk with delusions of literary grandeur. He was both. After his death, the manuscript of *Billy Budd* sat in a breadbox, known only to his family. It was published posthumously, thirty-five years later. Melville died like a kid cranking out an irregular poetry zine with a novel in his drawer.

* * *

NO WHINING. IT doesn't help and it's probably wrong. You don't know what forces are shaping your future. Nobody does. The legend of John Keats is that he was killed by rejection, by bad reviews. Certainly, after his death, his friends and editors promoted him that way. Byron wrote:

'Tis strange the mind, that very fiery particle
Should let itself be snuffed out by an article.

But the legend of Keats's death by review can't withstand much scrutiny. Keats wrote to his brother a few months after the brutal reviews of *Endymion*, that "I think I shall be among the English poets after my death." Like Melville, Keats prevaricated between certainty of glory and a sense of total futility. After he saw bright arterial blood on his handkerchief during a coughing fit—from his surgical training, he knew it was a death sentence—his writerly existence became pure negative capability, the sense of all that he could have meant but didn't. "If I should die I have left no immortal work behind me—nothing to make my friends proud of my memory—but I have loved the principle of beauty in all things, and if I had had time I would have made myself remember'd," he wrote to Fanny Brawne before composing his own epitaph: "Here Lies One Whose Name was writ in Water." It was his friends who gave those words cover: "This Grave contains all that was Mortal of a Young English Poet Who, on his Death Bed, in the Bitterness of his Heart at the Malicious Power of his Enemies Desired these Words to be engraven on his Tomb Stone: Here lies One Whose Name was writ in Water." Keats's phrasing is more accurate than his friends', and more elegant, too. The oblivion Keats feared was not that the work he had written would perish but that the work he had not yet written would never be born.

As Keats lay dying by the Spanish Steps, he could hear, from his window, among the clatter of the street, the bubbling continuities of the nearby Fountain of the Sunken Boat, and there, every breath an agony, he "dreamed of a new poem, fusing the fountain with the brook he had leaned over as a boy, a dedication to the river-goddess Sabrina from Milton's Comus." It could have been the greatest poem ever written, except that it has failed to exist.

In 2004, astronomers identified a planet, 55 Cancri e, circling a star forty-one light years from our own, twice the size of Earth, and composed entirely of diamond.

That diamond planet, could we ever reach it, would not be an adequate compensation for the poem Keats died before writing.

* * *

IF IT WAS that way for Keats, why should it be any different for you? Every time you attempt anything other than a revamped version of a massive success, you can expect the process to be next to impossible. Don't complain. It should not be surprising that it's hard to sell your feelings. What's surprising is that there are sometimes buyers. With any distance from this process, with any perspective whatsoever on the business of writing, the status games that consume literary careers quickly dissolve into absurdity. The accountancy is pure distortion, at best a partial and temporary ledger-keeping.

Who thinks they're a success and who thinks they're a failure has nothing to do with success or failure. F. Scott Fitzgerald and Ernest Hemingway met, for the first time, at the Dingo Bar in the Rue Delambre in Paris, April 1925. They had a typical first meeting between writers, engaging in mild flattery, trying to impress each other, and drinking until one of them passed out. (In this case, Fitzgerald.) Fitzgerald thought of himself as a failure, even though, by that time, he had published *This Side of Paradise*, *The Beautiful and Damned*, *The Great Gatsby*, *Flappers and Philosophers*, and *Tales of the Jazz Age*, several of which were bestsellers. Ernest Hemingway was utterly convinced of his success even though his entire published output at that juncture consisted of 470 copies of two volumes totalling eighty-eight pages.

Often relationships between writers devolve into dick-measuring contests. In the case of Hemingway and Fitzgerald, it literally did. After his wife complained that his penis was too small to satisfy her, Fitzgerald asked Hemingway to take a look. Hemingway wrote the whole humiliating scene down, as Fitzgerald must have known he would. "'Forget what Zelda said,' I told him. 'Zelda is crazy. There's nothing wrong with you. Just have confidence and do what the girl wants. Zelda just wants to destroy you.'" Later, the critic Edmund Wilson recalled a New York dinner he shared with them. Fitzgerald was disgustingly drunk, passed out again.

> When Scott was lying in the corner on the floor, Hemingway said, Scott thinks that his penis is too small. (John Bishop had told me this and said that Scott was in the habit of making this assertion to anybody he met—to the lady who sat next to him for the first time.) I explained to him, Hemingway continued, that it only seemed to him small because he looked at it from above. You have to look at it in a mirror. (I did not understand this.)

Here is the perfect allegory of the comparison of literary careers. The size of your dick depends on the angle you hold the mirror.

It's a question of projection, of confidence. Hemingway was always a success to himself. Even his failures were successes. He told Fitzgerald once that "it was a good thing to publish a lousy book once in a while." Hemingway wrote poorly for whole decades without any hitch in his swagger. "Scott Fitzgerald was a failure as a success—and a failure as a failure," said the celebrated restaurateur Michael Romanoff. Even Fitzgerald's successes, in his own estimation were preludes to failures. "It was always the becoming he dreamed of, never the being," he wrote, and while he was speaking about one of his characters, he might as well have been speaking about himself.

Hemingway accepted Fitzgerald as a failure and Fitzgerald accepted Hemingway as a success. Their personae reflected their convictions: Hemingway out snagging marlins and blasting lions, then knocking back daiquiris beside a swimming pool full of movie stars. Fitzgerald broadcasting to the world he couldn't satisfy his wife, passed out in the corner. They each got what they thought they were going to get, as so often happens. During the year of his death, all of Fitzgerald's books combined sold seventy-two copies. Hemingway won the Nobel Prize.

In the end, though, how much difference was there between them? Both wrote masterpieces. Both committed suicide, Hemingway with a shotgun and Fitzgerald with a bottle. Meanwhile, they used each other to define themselves. "I talk with the authority of failure—Ernest with the authority of success," Fitzgerald remembered, but that authority was auto-generated. The first fictions writers create are the fiction of the writers they become. Realistic self-assessment is the first victim of a life making meaning.

* * *

WHAT ASSESSMENT IS reasonable, though? Whose assessment? On what terms? At what point in time? If you take the career of, say, Ezra Pound in the middle of his life, who was ever bigger, more successful? Putting aside his own work—the early imagist lyrics, *The Cantos*, the translations from the Chinese—Pound was easily the most influential editor of the twentieth century. He turned the wasteland into *The Waste Land*. He helped to find a publisher for *Ulysses* after nobody else could. He told Hemingway to be sparing with adjectives and suggested to E. E. Cummings that he might fool around with typewritten layout. In the middle of his life, he was the key to the meaning of the century. By the end of his life, he was a caution, a monster of nowhere and nothing, emptiness embodied.

By the time the Allies captured Pound, in May of 1945, he had given over two hundred radio broadcasts in support of the Italian fascist regime, speaking on the side of the Nazis even after the U.S. Department of Justice indicted him for treason. The month of his capture, he described Hitler as "a martyr" and Mussolini as "a very human, imperfect character who lost his head." Pound's seventy-second and seventy-third cantos are fascist works. The seventy-third celebrates a peasant woman leading a company of Canadian soldiers to their death in a minefield.

His captors stuffed him in a "gorilla cage," six by six, at the edge of a dusty, glaring field. Eventually, he was permitted the use of a typewriter. He wrote:

No one who has passed a month in the death cells
    believes in capital punishment
No man who has passed a month in the death cells
    believes in cages for beasts

The heat and isolation led to what was described, in that time, as "a nervous breakdown." Though he was not insane—no doctor could find evidence of psychosis—the authorities relegated him to St. Elizabeth's lunatic asylum, the government hospital outside Washington, DC, mainly because they had no idea what else to do with him. Ezra Pound became number 58102.

St. Elizabeth's was not to be his worst humiliation. After twelve and a half years, the US government released Pound, and he returned to Italy. In 1967, Allen Ginsberg visited him in Venice. At that moment, Ginsberg was central to culture in a way few poets in history have ever been. *Howl* had sold over a million copies. Multiple distinct subcultures were emanating from Ginsberg's work and celebrity—hipsterism, ersatz Western Buddhism, drug culture. Pound's fundamental dictum, maybe the basic principle of modernism itself, was clarity: "Fundamental accuracy of statement is the ONE sole morality of writing," he had written. Ginsberg was the opposite, a slob in every sense, his poetry devoted not to control and mastery, but to chaos and a vague narcissism packaged and hustled as elevation of the spirit.

Literature can be understood as the meeting of those who would never meet otherwise. You have Pound, neat, his elegant suit pressed, hat and cane in hand, his eyes black coals of crushed spirit and intense consideration. You have Ginsberg, bald and bushy, with a dazed acid-inflected smile on his goofy lips. During their first meeting, Ginsberg forced Pound to listen to Bob Dylan and the Beatles, expounding their cosmic relevance. Enduring this hippie nonsense would be tough going for anyone; for Pound, it must have been torture. Pound could uniquely understand the charlatanism on display—the illiterate stoner's understanding of Eastern mysticism, the latest pop music taken as Beethoven. It's not every man who gets to meet a parody of his best self. Even worse, Ginsberg, the grubby little blabbermouth, who embodied so much that Pound despised, obviously worshipped him. He had sent many letters to Pound during his tenure at St. Elizabeth's. It's not like Pound could just tell him to fuck off.

They later had dinner in the restaurant of the Pensione Cici. Ginsberg wanted to discuss *The Cantos*, which he adored in his blithering way. Pound disagreed:

> "A mess," he said.
>
> "What, you or the *Cantos* or me?"
>
> "My writing—stupidity and ignorance all the way through," he said, "Stupidity and ignorance ... The intention was bad—that's the trouble—anything I've done has been an accident—any good has been spoiled by my intentions—the preoccupation with irrelevant and stupid things—" Pound said this quietly, rusty voiced like an old child, looking directly in my eye while pronouncing "intention."
>
> "Ah well, what I'm trying to tell you—what I came here for all this time—was to give you my blessing then, because despite your disillusion—unless you want to be a messiah—then you have to be a Buddhist to be the perfect Messiah," (he smiled) "—But I'm a Buddhist Jew, perceptions have been strengthened by the series of practical exact language models which are scattered throughout the *Cantos* like stepping stones—ground for me to occupy, walk on—so that despite your intentions

the practical effect has been to clarify my percep-
tions—and anyway, now, do you accept my
blessing?"

He hesitated, opening his mouth like an old tur-
tle. "I do," he said "—but my worst mistake was the
stupid suburban prejudice of anti-Semitism, all
along, that spoiled everything."

And so Pound offered his confession to and received the
benediction of a drug-addled, homosexual Jewish hippie
with no taste. His life had become a scene out of Dante:
The blessing a fulfillment of a curse, the crime its punishment, the work its own emptiness. The master of meaning
had fallen into the deepest possible miscomprehension.

The punishment for treason is death. For writers,
there are more permanent punishments.

* * *

THE WORLD DOES not particularly like writers. It never
has. They celebrate a few, for reasons of their own, but
they allow most to rot and die, and for every one they
celebrate, they persecute a hundred. The ancient Romans
understood persecution better than the rest. They knew
how to afflict others and their own. They didn't execute
Ovid, their greatest poet. They consigned him to irrelevance. Nobody quite knows why. *Carmen et error*, a poem
and a mistake, was the official explanation, which
explained nothing. He said something he shouldn't have
and he fucked somebody he shouldn't have, probably. The
emperor banished Ovid to Tomis, a colony in present-day
Romania. Among barbarians, far from friends, far from

the pleasures of civilization, the cruelty was that he no longer had a say. You know what Ovid did? You know what the greatest Roman poet of them all did? He started to write poems in the language of the barbarians, in Getic. He wrote a eulogy for Augustus, the emperor who exiled him, in Getic. Getic has disappeared. Ovid's poem has disappeared with it. Those Romans knew what they were doing. Death would have been a dawdle.

* * *

LEGALLY IMPOSED IRRELEVANCE, like Ovid's, is rare. The standard method of destroying writers is casual indifference. If you had to pick one writer from all of history it would be Ovid, but if you had to pick two, they would be eighth century poets Li Bai and Du Fu, first flowers of the Tang Dynasty, the most elegant voices of the most elegant period in literate culture. A soft, swelling indifference overwhelmed their lives, indifference like a tumbling fog.

In the rambling failures of their lives, the two master poets shared geography only once. They met in Hunan province, after Li Bai had dissipated himself out of court and Du Fu had failed the imperial examinations. Li Bai, the elder, was in his early forties, Du Fu thirty-two. If there is one activity that defines the life of a writer other than writing, it is borrowing money to drink, and while Chinese scholars dispute who was the greater poet, Li Bai or Du Fu, with the decision weighing slightly in favour of Du Fu, at cadging drinks Li Bai can never be topped. After his friend Ho Chih-chang died, Li Bai memorialized the booze:

I remember how once he pawned his golden tortoise
To buy me wine, and tears wet my scarf.

Li Bai never managed a household of his own. Li Bai
never even sat the imperial examinations. Li Bai had no
title to write after his name. Li Bai was a "person in plain
clothes." The emperor briefly set him up at Han-lin Acad-
emy, a kept man taken out whenever a court member
needed encomia. The gig was sweet: "I rode a colt from
the Emperor's stable, my stripes were of filigree, my sad-
dle was studded with white jade, my bed was of ivory, my
mat of fine silk. I ate out of a golden dish." Gigs like that
never last. His life was a drunkard's, careening down the
streets, bumping into thorns and mercy.

The banished immortal was perpetually broke. At
Kuikang, in a misunderstanding, the authorities arrested
him for treason but he caught a break. The assistant
director of the Censorate, a poetry-lover, happened to be
passing and freed him. But even powerful men who
wanted to help him couldn't. You don't give top admin-
istrative positions to falling-down drunks even if they're
brilliant. The emperor banished Li Bai to Hunan, and the
officials who saw him off in the boat left him "lying
drunk all alone."

In Hunan province, meeting Li Bai, Du Fu still had
hopes left to shatter. Together, with their mutual friend
Kao She, the poets climbed to the Terrace of Ch'ui T'ai
and "drank wine, sang songs in a mournful tone and
thought of ancient days." Du Fu taught Li Bai to eat a
peasant dish, rice dried in the sun, steeped in the juices
of the pressed leaves of heavenly bamboo. Together, they
wandered the mountains, searching for a hermit scholar,

who had either retired from the world so successfully that he couldn't be found or was a legend, a dream of retirement busy men had dreamed. Together, in the mountains, they would discuss the difficulties of poetry as they picked burrs off their hiking clothes.

Their friendship was a gift of recognition. The world existed as a subject. Leaves whirled together in a courtyard. Notes dropped by ladies in the mud. The women along the winter streams beat laundry with batons so that they would have lines to write about them. The mountains rose through the mists as a repudiation of their vanity. The frost fanned across the marshes, and the mulberry leaves tumbled like sleet in the weed-flustered air so that they could see the beauty of the passage. They served as registrars of the universe in the gloom of obscurity. They saw each other. Du Fu wrote:

> I declare I love Li Bai
> the way I would a brother
>
> it's autumn, we get drunk
> and share a bed to sleep it off.

In the autumn, Du Fu left to try his luck in the capital. They were whirled together, then whirled apart.

Du Fu's life was steadier in its decline than Li Bai's, misbegotten from beginning to end. He was descended from eleven generations of scholars but failed the imperial examinations twice, once in his youth and once in a year the emperor passed no one. During the rebellion of An Lushan, he recorded the conscripts going to far fields to die, recorded their families dissolving, their sons and daughters dead from sheer hunger. He found himself stuck in the capital with traitors, far from his own wife and children. At the Restoration, he was given a longed-for government post, but as an omissioner, pointing out to the emperor errors in ritual and tradition, a painful task for which he was never paid. Refused and rescinded, he drifted with his family five hundred miles south to Brocade City, where he built a thatched hut for himself, to starve in dignity. There, without any hope of any kind, he found a miserable happiness:

> I no longer hear from friends
> who live on princely salaries
>
> my children are always hungry
> with pale and famished faces
>
> does a madman grow more happy
> before he dies in the gutter?

He titled that poem "I Am a Madman."

By the time he died, Li Bai had been a refugee for eight years. He drowned, so they said, reaching for the moon's reflection in the drunken waters. Lunatic: So they said. In some accounts, Du Fu died in a boat on the Yangtze River. They had that season together. They each had the resonance of the other.

If Li Bai and Du Fu drowned in their irrelevance, why would it be any different for you?

* * *

THE GREATEST HISTORIAN of all time had his balls hacked off. That should tell you all you need to know about how much the world respects history. Without Sima Qian, the Grand Historian, there would be only scant records of the dynasties of the Qin and the Han, hundreds of years in unknowingness. In the first century BCE, poorly expressed advice to the emperor led to a sentence of castration for Sima Qian. Traditionally the sentence of castration, for men the most humiliating punishment available, the "punishment of rottenness," was a formality; you were supposed to kill yourself rather than endure the degrada- tion. Sima Qian decided not to kill himself, as he would very much have preferred to do. He needed to live in order to finish his history. "When I have truly completed this work, I will deposit it in the Famous Mountain archives," he wrote to his confidante Ren An. "If it may be handed down to those who will appreciate it and pen- etrate to the villages and great cities, then though I should suffer a thousand mutilations, what regret would I have?" I'm appalled at how recognizable his pain is across the span of two thousand years:

> Though a hundred generations pass, my defilement will only become greater. That is the thought that wrenches my bowels nine times each day. Sitting at home, I am befuddled as though I had lost some- thing; I go out and then realize that I do not know where I am going. Each time I think of this shame, the sweat pours from my back and soaks my robe.

At the current moment, heroism has been confused with victimhood, and the writing store always has victims in stock, a pile of mangled corpses, testicles and tongues slivered onto bloody floors, shot at dawn for no reason. Writers tend to be tortured second, right after the political organizers. Insofar as there is heroism to writing, it is Sima Qian's heroism: To persevere through the condition of total rejection, so that the work may come to be, to keep throwing yourself against the door so that a crack may allow light in. That is what strength, in this business, looks like.

* * *

I DO NOT believe that suffering exalts. I do not believe that what doesn't kill you makes you stronger. I do not believe in the dignity of poverty. It is nonetheless true that some of the greatest works rise out of the worst horrors. Glories stroll out of burning buildings.

The Prince would never have come to be if Niccolò Machiavelli had not been defeated and tortured. In 1513, he lost his job as second chancellor of Florence— "dismissed, deprived and totally removed," the city decreed—after the Medicis overthrew the Florentine Republic. The citizen militia Machiavelli had spent his life constructing fled at first contact with mercenaries. He was on the side of history's losers.

His arrest and detention at Le Stinche prison involved the strappado. The torturers bound Machiavelli's hands behind his back at the wrists, walked him up a platform where they tied that rope to a second rope on the wall, hoisted him up, and by repeatedly dropping him, trussed up, tore his tendons and dislocated his joints. Machiavelli endured six sessions with the strappado. Only good luck saved him. The pope died, and Giovanni de' Medici snagged the job, and in celebration the Medicis ordered a mass release of prisoners. In *The Prince*, Machiavelli explicitly warns against acts of generosity like the one that spared his own life.

He recovered from torture in squalor. "Thus I will remain," he wrote to his friend Vettori in 1514, "crawling with lice, unable to find a solitary man who recalls my service or believes I might be good for anything. But it is impossible for me to continue like this, because I am coming apart at the seams and I can see that if God does not show me more favour, one day I shall be forced to leave my home and find a place as a tutor or secretary to a governor, if I can find nothing else, or exile myself to some deserted land to teach reading to children. As if already dead, I will leave my family behind. They will do much better without me because I am nothing but an expense." Instead of teaching reading to kids, he wrote *The Prince*. From the darkest impotence, he set forth his manifesto of effectiveness. *The Prince* is a guide to gaining and maintaining power written out of the failure to gain or maintain power.

Machiavelli is the ultimate example of "Those who can't do, teach." It's like you blew an opponent away in tennis and then he came to the net and offered to show you a few pointers. Machiavelli taught Lorenzo de' Medici that "The end justifies the means" and "It's better to be feared than loved" but Lorenzo had already demon-strated, amply, that he understood those principles. "Remember that time I had you tortured?" the Medici might have asked. "I guess I know something about power that you don't." Machiavelli had some chutzpah.

But it's a chutzpah that extends across the field of political writing. Anyone who is merely writing about power isn't wielding power.

There's also this to consider: It's not like Lorenzo de' Medici could have written *The Prince* any more than Machiavelli could have been the prince. No grand emperor, no transformative revolutionary, no master politician ever wrote a better book about power than *The Prince*. Maybe you can only know how power works after it's strung you up from the ceiling and dropped you to break you.

* * *

BROKENNESS AS INSIGHT. I don't want to believe it but I might have to. The world cracks some writers and their yolks fall right into the pan. In 1849, the Russian authorities arrested Fyodor Dostoevsky for his involvement in the Petrashevsky Circle. "I can add nothing new to my defence," he told the Commission of Inquiry, "except perhaps this—that I never acted with an evil and premeditated intention against the government—what I did was done thoughtlessly and much almost accidentally, as for example my reading of Belinsky's letter." His punishment for thoughtless, accidental dissidence was to be an inconceivable cruelty and a magnificent gift. The Russian authorities gave him the absurdity of the universe and the vulnerability of human beings. They gave him a cosmic trembling. Then he turned that trembling into Dostoevsky.

The sentence for Dostoevsky and the conspirators was death. So they were told. In fact, the sentence was mock death, an established punishment in nineteenth-century

Russia—If the czar commuted your sentence, the law called for a ceremonial execution and redemption. Typically, the ceremony was a formality. In Dostoevsky's case, under the czar's specific instructions, the mock execution was played straight. The Petrashevsky Circle was to be made to believe in their execution.

So on December 22 the guards led Dostoevsky out of his cell, returned his clothes to him, and handed him a pair of fresh warm socks. In the dim early-morning light, a frost-blinded carriage carried him to Semenovsky Square, white with fresh snow. The sun was rising—Dostoevsky wouldn't have seen it for eight months—illuminating a scaffold a couple of stories high, limned with black crepe. An official quickly ordered the prisoners into lines. A priest carrying a cross led them to the scaffold before an array of troops. Dostoevsky found himself beside his friend Mombelli, and he blurted out the plan of a story he'd been writing in prison. A soldier barked at them to remove their hats. The other soldiers ripped the hats off more hesitant heads. A civil servant, in full dress uniform, moved down the line of prisoners reciting, to each, in turn, their crimes and punishments, but so rapidly and mechanically that none of them could make out what he was saying. They heard one line all right: "The Field Criminal Court has condemned all to death before a firing squad."

Dostoevsky turned to his old friend Durov. "It's not possible that we'll be executed." Durov pointed to a nearby peasant cart, filled with coffins on straw matting. The officials handed out fresh white shirts. The priest held out a Bible: "Brothers! Before dying one must repent ... The Saviour forgives the sins of those who repent ... I call you to confession." Soldiers began strapping the first three men—Petrashevsky, Mombelli, Grigoryev—to stakes beside the scaffold, placing nightcaps over their heads. Petrashevsky refused the nightcap. He wanted to see death. The firing squad raised their rifles. They awaited the order to fire.

Everyone waited for the order. For a minute they waited. They waited for the volley. They waited for the death they knew was coming. They kept waiting.

The drums beat a retreat. The soldiers lowered their rifles.

An aide-de-camp galloped into the square, bringing the czar's pardon. Two men in executioner's clothing climbed the scaffold, forced the prisoners to their knees, and ritualistically broke swords over their heads.

The moment he arrived back at the prison, Dostoevsky wrote his brother Mikhail. His first thought, after nearly being executed, was its effect on his writing. "Can it be that I will never again take my pen in hand? I think it will be possible in four years," he wrote. "My God! How many forms, still alive and created by me anew, will perish, extinguished in my brain or dissolved like poison in my bloodstream. Yes, if it's impossible to write I will die. Better fifteen years' imprisonment with pen in hand!" At the moment of supreme crisis, he was worried about his literary career.

The scene of mock execution is pure Dostoevsky—the wavering out on the precipice. On Semenovsky Square, life revealed itself as a cruel prank, absurdly formal and maliciously merciful, a farce undertaken at the behest of a distant majesty with a perverse sense of humour and an elaborate indifference. Consciousness could only be a miracle, a divinity, but subject to the fragility of bare existence—the human figure flush with imagined power and total impotence.

The mock execution had different effects on different people. Grigoryev broke down raving. The authorities declared him a mental invalid. Dostoevsky wrote *The Idiot*. The authorities declared him a genius.

* * *

A DISQUIETING POSSIBILITY: It may be that the best work forms itself in degradation and fear. Anna Akhmatova, the Russian poet, lived a merry bright youth with seasons at the Summer Palace and portraits by Modigliani in Paris. She wrote banalities during all that merry brightness. The work that counted, the work that mattered, came out of the pure anguish of Stalinism. Anguished technique may be superior to merry brightness.

During the purges, Akhmatova lived on the charity of others in the "cesspit of communal homes," after having been expelled from the writers' union and forgoing her food ration card. Surveillance by the state was so total that she would place a hair in her notebooks to see if anyone had entered her house to read them, even though she would only ever dare to jot down banalities. While she survived barely, cooking in borrowed pots, cobbling together borrowed mittens and borrowed boots to equip her son for the gulag, she continued to write. She persevered even though she could literally not put words down on paper.

Her friend Lydia Chukovskaya described the unique process of the composition of Akhmatova's masterpiece, *Requiem*. The poet had to write down her lines and have her friends memorize them before destroying any record of their composition.

> Suddenly in mid-conversation, she would fall silent, and signaling me with her eyes at the ceiling and walls, she would get a scrap of paper and a pencil; then she would loudly say something very mundane, "Would you like some tea?" then she would cover the scrap in hurried handwriting and pass it to me. I would read the poems, and having memorized them, would hand them back to her in silence. "How early the autumn came this year," Anna Andreevna would say loudly and, striking a match would burn the paper over an ashtray.

Editing the text was as impossible as writing it. Akhmatova had to call her friends back in and have them re-memorize passages. She would insist on her precise wording. Old versions were to be forgotten. The technique, necessary to prevent any record of any kind that any secret policeman could abuse, fused oral and print modes of composition to produce a unique masterpiece. "We live according to the slogan 'Down with Gutenberg,'" she liked to say. The lines had to be memorable to survive. Any changes, since they were so painful, had to be essential and final. Which is why every word of *Requiem* is perfect. The words fit together like the stones in the Machu Picchu walls that need no mortar because of the precision of their carving and placement. It was the worst possible way to write. It was also the best possible way to write.

* * *

"BAD FORTUNE, I think, is more use to a man than good fortune," Boethius wrote in the sixth century. "Good fortune always seems to bring happiness, but deceives you with her smiles, whereas bad fortune is always truthful because by changing she shows her true fickleness. Good fortune deceives, but bad fortune enlightens. With her display of specious riches good fortune enslaves the minds of those who enjoy her, while bad fortune gives men release through the recognition of how fragile a thing happiness is." Boethius ought to have known, I guess. He wrote *The Consolation of Philosophy* after some trumped-up connection to a plot against the Goth Emperor Theodoric led to his imprisonment and condemnation to death. Up to that moment, he'd been a lucky guy, a prominent member of a patrician family, a prodigy, head of the whole Roman civil service for a while. His two sons became consuls on the same day—honour enough for any life. Only after his fall could he write *The Consolation*. They tortured Boethius by tying a cord around his temples and pulling until his eyes popped out of his head before they cudgelled him to death. Was that enough bad luck for him? If you do need bad luck to write, how much do you need?

* * *

IT'S STUPID TO say that writers need to suffer. The biographies of writers do not fit a collective pattern, not even of suffering. You got your martyrs. You got your lucky bastards. You got your drunks. You got your teetotalers. You got your libertines. You got your prudes. You got your assholes. You got your sweethearts. You've got murderers, murder victims, rapists, rape victims, police. You got

people who are good with money. You got people who are
bad with money. You got cheats. You got junkies. You got
guys who live good portions of their lives in whorehouses.
You've got guys who never recover from the shock of dis-
covering that women have pubic hair. You got devoted
parents. You got deadbeats. You got people who could
never imagine having kids. You got old ladies in the jun-
gle. You got teenagers who throw their talents away so
they can wander the desert. You got weird sisters who
converse in a private language around sooty fireplaces.
You got German lunatics clinging to the necks of beaten-
to-death horses in the street. The only substantial truth
of human behaviour applies, with double force, to the
lives of writers: It depends.

So anyone who tells you that you have to be a certain
way to be a writer, that you have to live a certain life, that
you have to see the world or that you have to lock yourself
away, that you have to abandon your people or that you
have to love your people, that you have to suffer or that
you have to forget your suffering, whatever, it's all bullshit. You have to write. You have to submit. You have to
persevere. You have to throw yourself against the door.
That's it.

* * *

THERE DOES EXIST writing without perseverance,
although it's rare and such is the nature of the enterprise
that to write without perseverance requires its own kind
of perseverance. Success is an attire; sometimes it slows
you down if it grows too heavy. "Celebrity, even the mod-
est sort that comes to writers, is an unhelpful exercise in

self-consciousness," John Updike wrote. "One can either see or be seen. Most of the best fiction is written out of early impressions, taken in before the writer became conscious of himself as a writer. The best seeing is done by the hunted and the hunter, the vulnerable and the hungry; the 'successful' writer acquires a film over his eyes. His eyes get fat. Self-importance is a thickened, occluding form of self-consciousness. The binge, the fling, the trip—all attempt to shake the film and get back under the dining room table, with a child's beautifully clear eyes." Add another contradiction to the business of writing: Success destroys what gives success.

In the United States, after the Second World War, there was a peculiar phenomenon, pretty much unknown in any other place or time, of career-ending literary triumph. It happened more than once. After *Invisible Man*, Ralph Ellison became more than a writer; he served as a sort of fusion of political and artistic achievement for whom mere composition of manuscripts seemed like some quaint old-world ritual. He could have written a shit book on toilet paper, and they would have published it. He couldn't. Success silenced him. He left behind, from the second half of his life, only some loose notes no editor has ever been able to turn into a cohesive work.

Joseph Mitchell, the *New Yorker* writer, finished his masterpiece, "Joe Gould's Secret," in 1964. He came into the office regularly for the next thirty-two years and contributed not one word to the magazine. Calvin Trillin remembered hearing that Mitchell lived "writing away at a normal pace until some professor called him the greatest living master of the English declarative sentence and stopped him cold." Acclaim ended these writers' work, as it did with Harper Lee and J. D. Salinger.

* * *

WITHOUT STRUGGLE THERE is the struggle of no struggle. They call it writer's block.

Writer's block begins as writers start to take themselves seriously. The first recorded instance was of Samuel Taylor Coleridge, in his early thirties. A friend told him to pull himself together and put something down on paper. "You bid me rouse myself," he answered. "Go, bid a man paralytic in both arms rub them briskly together, and that will cure him. Alas! (he would reply) that I cannot move my arms is my complaint." There used to be another phrase for writer's block. It used to be called "not having anything to say."

* * *

I SOMETIMES WONDER if writer's block should be received as a blessing. It's treated as a pathology, a disease. Maybe it's a sign of health, or at least of a cure taking. It's the writer's brain saying, "You don't need to do this anymore. Go do something else with your life." If writing involves failure in its essence, is not-writing the final sign of success?

* * *

ANOTHER WAY OF putting the question is, Does writing require a state of perseverance? What did J. K. Rowling do after she found herself lord and master over a multi-billion-dollar story empire? She gave herself the name Robert Galbraith, she wrote a novel under that name, she submitted, she published, she sold modestly, she persevered. She even posted the rejections, in order, she claimed, to inspire kid writers. What was the inspiration? It was a mediocre book by an unknown name. What other reaction would there be? The whole affair was an exercise in pure ego. I imagine she wanted to test her talents against the marketplace. But the marketplace doesn't test talent. It tests timing.

Some of the most successful writers develop a *nostalgie de la boue*, a craving for the gutter. Alex Haley, the author of *Roots*, lived the standard life of total rejection for many years. He remembered the phrasing of one rejection note from *Reader's Digest*: "'Dear Mr. Haley: We're sorry, but this does not quite jell for us.'" Years later, after *Roots* was adapted for television, Haley found himself on the *Reader's Digest* corporate jet. "Outside it, two men with crew cuts, gray pants, blue coats, brass buttons, and the *Digest* logo. I walked up the runway into the plane, and I looked around at seats for about fourteen people, but there was nobody but me. One of the men came up and said, 'Sir, if you'd like, there's scotch, bourbon, cigars, cigarettes' and there was everything. There was a silver tray with all kinds of little sandwiches cut in circles, diamonds, and everything." What did he contemplate at this moment of triumph? "Then, back to me came the thing I associated with *Reader's Digest*. I remembered those rejection slips and what they said. And the thought just came to me. 'Well, I guess it finally jelled.'" Even in the face of massive success, a little part, maybe a big part, maybe the biggest part of the writer's heart, dwells in failure.

* * *

ALEXANDR SOLZHENITSYN SURVIVED partisan warfare against the Nazis, then the gulag, then cancer. He wrote brilliantly about each misery. The United States harboured him in 1974, offering him freedom, security, and medical care. He loathed the West that had saved him. The culture was pornography. The media was empty gossip. The politics was what you could get away with. "Hastiness and superficiality are the psychic disease of the 20th century," Solzhenitsyn told an audience at Harvard. The freedom, so long hungered for, turned to emptiness in his guts. The moment he could return to the country that had tortured and condemned him, he went. For many writers, home is where the suffering is.

* * *

WRITERS DO HAVE, it can't be denied, a higher propensity to mental illness than ordinary people. A study of all poets reviewed in the *New York Times Book Review* between 1960 and 1990 revealed that 18 percent had committed suicide. *Touched with Fire*, Kay Redfield Jamison's 1993 study of writing and mental illness, compiled anecdotes on the mental conditions of hundreds of writers between 1705 and 1805 (so before the advent of the Romantic connection between madness and genius) and found they were about five times more likely to kill themselves than the general population and thirty times more likely to be symptomatic of general mood disorders. Researchers attempted to analyze the mental health of contemporary writers by testing participants from the University of Iowa Writer's Workshop. They found 80 percent of the sample "met formal diagnostic criteria for a major mood disorder." In 2013, a much broader sample, over a million subjects, found good news for creatives generally: "Except for bipolar disorder, individuals with overall creative professions were not more likely to suffer from investigated psychiatric disorders than controls." They had some bad news for writers, though: "Being an author was specifically associated with increased likelihood of schizophrenia, bipolar disorder, unipolar depression, anxiety disorders, substance abuse, and suicide."

Personally I've never been attracted to the notion of mad genius. My own life has been an almost comically exaggerated exercise in normalcy—marriage, two kids, mortgage, shitty car. I have tried to live by Flaubert's advice: "Be regular and orderly in your life like a bourgeois, so that you may be violent and original in your work." There's also the matter that several of my closest friends have gone insane, and I have found zero romance in their struggles with mental illness. It is affliction, debilitation. The same goes for the romance of alcohol and drugs as spurs to creativity; that shit is strictly for the tourists, pure shtick. Serious alcoholic writers, and there are and have been plenty, know that booze takes writing just like it takes everything else.

Suicide is a risk in this profession the way that losing a finger is a risk if you work in a sawmill; it is something that must be protected against. "We do not know our own souls, let alone the souls of others," Virginia Woolf wrote. "Human beings do not go hand in hand the whole stretch of the way. There is a virgin forest in each; a snowfield where even the print of birds' feet is unknown. Here we go alone, and like it better so." The madness that came over Woolf was not a gift of meaning but a flood of meaninglessness. "I feel certain I am going mad again. I feel we can't go through another of those terrible times. And I shan't recover this time. I begin to hear voices, and I can't concentrate. So I am doing what seems the best thing to do," she wrote in her suicide note. I've never seen any evidence that has convinced me that the mood disorders that lead to suicidal ideation drive creativity. It's possible, I guess, that the act of writing and the business of writing contribute to the desire for death, but it's impossible to tell how or why. Suicide ideation is a sickness. It's not part of the creative process. Virginia Woolf's family tree is a series of recurrent depressives, bipolar sufferers and unspecified psychotics. None of them wrote *To the Lighthouse*. None of them killed themselves either. How and why creativity connects with mental ill health is fundamentally mysterious.

* * *

READERS LOVE SUICIDES. There's no point denying it. The market loves to see writers kill themselves. They want to see you bleed, any way you will. All mentions of David Foster Wallace, out of habit, begin with his suicide, and it's not hard to see why. Wallace's death had double prestige, first as a literary suicide, in the tradition of Hemingway and Woolf, and then as a rock 'n' roll suicide, in the tradition of Kurt Cobain. Artists who kill themselves are comforting in their familiarity. Suicide gives readers the sensation that the stakes of art are real.

Whether Wallace's creativity was the result of his psychological instability is, I suppose, one of the grand questions, but as far as I can tell from the study of his biography, the periods where the Nardil was working were the periods of real productivity. Quite simply, his death was the result of a psychopharmacological catastrophe: He didn't like the side effects of the medication he was on; he went off it and couldn't get back on. Those facts didn't matter. After his death, pop culture and high art clichés immediately elevated Wallace into the self-slaughtering martyrology.

Even in college, Wallace resisted the ancient cult of writerly melancholia. His biographer, D. T. Max, credits his proximity to real depression with dissuading him from the celebration of fantasy depression indulged by some of his friends. Still, he explored despair and suicide in much of his work, and he found it in odd places. In the essay that made Wallace famous, "A Supposedly Fun Thing I'll Never Do Again," he identified despair as the core of the cruise ship experience:

> The word's overused and banalified now, *despair*, but it's a serious word, and I'm using it seriously. For me it denotes a simple admixture—a weird yearning for death combined with a crushing sense of my own smallness and futility that presents as a fear of death. It's maybe close to what people call dread or angst. But it's not these things, quite. It's more like wanting to die in order to escape the

unbearable feeling of becoming aware that I'm
small and weak and selfish and going without any
doubt at all to die. It's wanting to jump overboard.

In Wallace, the white culture of consumerist garbage
emerged not as rage against an other, but as self-loathing.
The fury directed inward. He understood, absolutely, that
his luxurious despair was tied into his position as a consumerist white American man in the late twentieth
century. Suicide is the Romantic gesture for conformists.

In the popular imagination, the tortured soul of the
artist, after corralling his or her pain into glorious
achievements of the spirit, is finally, tragically overwhelmed by its unbearable source. The case of David
Foster Wallace poses a disturbing counterproposal: What
if the process flowed in the opposite direction? What if
one of the conditions of greatness is that the audience
needs to see you kill yourself? What if that is what the
readership demands in order to call you great? What if
suicide were merely another accidentally good career
move? Wallace saw the fraud of suicide, its status as
imago, yet he was not able to escape. He fought against
the consumption and the smoothness and the casual wor-
ship of the abnegation of life, but no matter how
clear-eyed, no matter how good a swimmer, no writer
escapes the currents of their time. In the end, you'll be in
some hotel, and *The End of the Tour* will come on TV, and
you'll watch it, and you'll think: Oh, yeah, that writer who
used to wear a bandana. How did he kill himself again?

* * *

IN WESTERN CULTURE, the act of suicide must be excused or punished, as pathology or as crime. In Japan, where the suicide taboo is nowhere near as strong, suicides become writerly statements, yoking together, in a final supreme gesture, the despair of writing and the despair of living as a writer.

Mishima Yukio committed seppuku, ritual self-disembowelment, in 1970. On one level his samurai death was unrelated to his writing. He had founded a small fascist organization, the Shield Society, devoted to defending the emperor. After raiding the headquarters of Japan's Self-Defence Force, and after his rousing speech to the troops wilted, he killed himself. His death may seem like a gesture of straight politics. The coup failed: He had to die. But before he undertook the raid, Mishima delivered to his publishers the finished manuscript of *The Decay of the Angel*, the story of a man who tries to kill himself and fails, a gesture of literature. Meaning-making led him to death.

Akutagawa Ryunosuke devoted his career to the notion of literature as a work of nature, worshipping the primitive in poetry. He compared the act of writing to animal noises. "All lyric poetry must have had its origin in such a cry," he wrote, "the cry of a male deer calling for his mate." His suicide note was therefore a kind of literary testament: "I am one of the human animals. But I seem to be losing the animal force. Witness the fact that I have lost my appetite for food and for women." Animals don't kill themselves though. Only a species capable of language can perform self-slaughter.

Dazai Osamu's writings have been described as one long suicide note. His actual suicide note, he wrote to his wife: "I'm not dying because I hate you—it's because I've come to hate writing." Has there ever been a clearer statement of the love of writing? Killing himself was the only way he could think to stop.

In all these cases, the connection between writing and suicide is clear, but the question remains: Did writing lead to their suicides? Did the paths of meaning they opened lead to their deaths? Or rather was suicide an occasion? It's an old question. Is it that miserable people are attracted to writing? Or is it that writing causes misery? Or is it that the life of the writer is inherently miserable? Or is it all of the above?

* * *

THERE IS ANOTHER breed of writer, the breed that breaks out rather than folds in. Writing kills them but by way of defiance. "I couldn't leave your beautiful world without saying goodbye to you who are condemned to live in it," Ken Saro-Wiwa wrote in a 1989 short story. "I'd like you to put this on my gravestone as an epitaph: 'Africa Kills Her Sun.' A good epitaph, eh? Cryptic. Definite. A stroke of genius, I should say. I'm sure you'll agree with me." Saro-Wiwa was one of the earliest members of MOSOP, the Movement for the Survival of the Ogoni People, devoted to self-determination and the struggle against Royal Dutch Shell. By 1993, the Nigerian military had arrested him. In 1995, they executed him. Saro-Wiwa wrote the story first, then he lived the defiance. Both were creative acts: To tell the truth, he had to submit to being killed.

The defiance need not take the form of political activism. In 1978, Jorge Luis Borges didn't protest the military junta in Argentina. He didn't rail against the nationalism taking over his country. On the day of the opening match of the 1978 World Cup, the spectacular coming-out party for the regime, he gave a lecture on literary immortality. Rather than revel in public fervour, he chose private introspection. His "fuck you" was less specific but more all-embracing.

Some writers become acts of defiance in themselves. In 1922, the Bengali writer Kazi Nazrul Islam became famous for his poem "Bidrohi" or "The Rebel": "I am the rebel eternal, I raise my head beyond this world, high, ever erect and alone!" He became even more famous the next year, after the British accused him of sedition. "I am a poet," he told the court. "I have been sent by God to express the unexpressed, to portray the unportrayed." His defiance was political but it was also cosmic. And he was the defiance he composed.

In every way you can name, to live as a writer is to be up against it.

* * *

DON'T GET ME wrong. This job breaks people even without oppression. It's like metal fatigue. There are limits to perseverance. A. M. Klein, the Jewish Canadian poet who wrote some of the most fascinating material ever produced in this country, suffered a complete breakdown in his early forties and never wrote again. He barely even spoke. He sat silently on his porch and the children who played on his street believed him to be deaf. His final major poem, "The Portrait of the Poet as Landscape," is a reckoning with despair and perseverance:

He suspects that something has happened, a law
been passed, a nightmare ordered. Set apart,
he finds himself, with special haircut and dress,
as on a reservation. Introvert.
He does not understand this; sad conjecture
muscles and palls thrombotic on his heart.

By the end, he affirms himself in his irrelevance:

These are not mean ambitions. It is already
    something
merely to entertain them. Meanwhile, he
makes of his status as zero a rich garland,
a halo of his anonymity,
and lives alone, and in his secret shines
like phosphorous. At the bottom of the sea.

In the poem, perseverance triumphs. In Klein's life, despair. Scholars demur on the cause of Klein's breakdown; they attribute it partially to overwork and partially to an underlying condition. Later Jewish Canadian writers— Irving Layton, Leonard Cohen, Mordecai Richler—pitied Klein or mocked him. I fear him. I fear him because I know what broke him—the North, the sheer irrelevance of Canadian life, the confrontation with oblivion implicit in living beside wilderness, the wilful indifference to talent that defines Canadian culture. Klein is the ghost that haunts me. There's a little silenced Klein sitting right now in one of the chambers of my heart.

* * *

AT THIS POINT, you're probably thinking, He just hasn't succeeded enough. He just hasn't got to the promised land. I've thought that, too, about myself, for most of my life. I don't believe it anymore. There is no promised land. There is only exile. Exile offers its own pleasures, though, its own opportunities.

At this moment, I have no idea whether I'm successful or not. That's the honest truth. There would be those who would find it ridiculous of me to consider myself a failure. I make a living from writing, and I don't even have to teach. I receive fan mail almost every day. Because of some recent ads for an audio series I made, I am regularly recognized on the street. Others would consider the idea that I might consider myself a successful writer equally ridiculous. I've barely been published internationally. I only earned out a couple of books. I alienated myself out of the literary community of my own country as quickly as possible. I am unprizeable. By no means can I do just what I like. I only work on what I believe in but that's a way of describing my own pride rather than any external achievement.

The confusion on my part is not fishing for compliments or a mere exercise in vanity. As I've proceeded deeper into the writer's life, I understand less and less what success looks like. Or rather success as an idea, as a scheme, as a system of meaning, is dissolving in my hands, floating away, losing itself, like a language you learned in high school that you can't speak anymore. Success on what terms? Success compared to what?

* * *

GOOD WRITERS OFFER advice. Great writers offer condolences. The internet is full of writerly advice. Some of it's even good, like Elmore Leonard's: "Never open a book with weather," "Avoid prologues," "Never use a verb other than 'said' to carry dialogue." Other writerly advice can be too obvious or even beyond your control. "When still a child, make sure you read a lot of books," Zadie Smith proffered whimsically. Margaret Atwood's is outright wacky but also the most practical: "Before every one of your readings, have a Fisherman's Friend." Lists of writing rules are very popular, like rules for life, and about as accurate. They both offer a comforting sense of a measure of control, of agency, of purpose.

James Baldwin had more basic counsel. He told the *Paris Review*: "Write. Find a way to keep alive and write. There is nothing else to say. If you are going to be a writer there is nothing I can say to stop you. If you're not going to be a writer nothing I can say will help you." There follows Baldwin's recipe for a career: "Discipline, love, luck, but, most of all, endurance." Discipline, love, luck can all be boiled down to endurance. They're just motivations for endurance. James Baldwin's writing advice can be summed up in a word: Persevere.

Rainer Maria Rilke's *Letters to a Young Poet* contains some real lousy advice, pathetic stuff about learning from your own heart and not listening to critics, but the man was right about this: "In the deepest hour of the night, confess to yourself that you would die if you were forbidden to write. And look deep into your heart where it spreads its roots, the answer, and ask yourself, must I write?" Do not write unless you have to. That's not down to some question of the inner spirit. That's because anything you hope to achieve by writing—fame, money, pleasure, improving the world—can always be achieved some better way than writing.

* * *

THE REASONS TO persevere don't have to be good. Writers, like everybody else, do the right things for the wrong reasons some, if not most, of the time. Total classics have been written so the writer could pay rent. Sacred creative intentions regularly lead to the dullest work imaginable. Recently, Jerry Saltz, the *New York* magazine art critic, advised against envy, speaking of his own all-consuming hatred for everyone slightly more successful than himself as the enemy of his own creative potential. His clarity about his own failings is admirable, but I'm not sure he's right, or rather I think he must be half wrong. Envy may be the soul-killer but it's often the art-giver. The impulse right at the beginning of an art career is envy, an encounter with beauty and power that twists itself into the thought: I wish I could do that. I wish I could be like that.

I've always been envious. With unfailing instinct, though, I've always envied the wrong things. In my twenties, I obsessed over the Journey Prize, the award they give every year to a Canadian short story. I convinced myself, for nearly a decade, that if I won the Journey Prize, it would be me and Michael Ondaatje discussing the North at Oxford a few weeks later. If I've matured in my career, it's only insofar as my envy has become more precise. I've seen enough to know that even big successes are mostly fleeting. You shouldn't envy any writer, not because it's bad for your soul but because it's stupid. You have no idea what people are going through. You have no idea how things will work out.

* * *

ENVY BETTER. BE scrupulous in your envy.

* * *

HERE'S THE THING: The sources of writerly perseverance are mostly silly. Samuel Johnson once said that "no man but a blockhead ever wrote except for money," but if you're looking to make money, there are a hundred thousand better ways to do it than writing. Still, the drive to survive financially is one of the greatest sources of writerly perseverance. "Where does a man get inspiration to write a song like that?" Grace Kelly asks in *Rear Window*, overhearing a neighbour's new melody. "He gets it from his landlady once a month," Jimmy Stewart answers. The very best reason to keep throwing yourself against the door is because you have to.

Sheer bloody-mindedness, too, is underrated as a motive. So much has been written in the spirit of "I'm going to show those motherfuckers." The problem with bloody-mindedness is that you never do get to show any of those motherfuckers. As I've mentioned, I've been rejected many thousands of times. I'm going to show all of them? Besides, if you do get to a point where you can show those motherfuckers, they've probably vanished. The people you want to prove wrong die. The institutions that you want revenge on dissolve. "Time is no healer,"

T. S. Eliot said. "The patient is no longer here." It is one of life's merciful little sadnesses.

* * *

THE MOTIVES OF perseverance, I think I should point out, are all probably stupid. Perseverance is a form of what the Buddhists call attachment. A life of blessed inconsequence is probably superior. Money and bloody-mindedness are better sources for perseverance than the love of writing, that's for sure. Writers are often proud of how much they hate writing. I find it bizarre. You don't hear guitar players whining about how much they hate playing the guitar. But the sheer joy of writing well, the affiliation with controlled language, the booming resonance of the Word to the horizon of being, the chance to play the glamorous instrument, English, the unsolvable labyrinth of tone and significance that lead to fleeting recognitions, apparent even in this miniature essay, to see that Li Bai and Herman Melville would have commiserated, to know that Ovid and James Baldwin walked in the same dark woods—that love of language won't keep you working.

* * *

"FAIL BETTER," SAMUEL Beckett commanded, a phrase that has been taken on by business executives as some kind of ersatz wisdom. They miss Beckett's point. Beckett didn't mean failure-on-the-way-to-delayed-success, which is what the FailCon crowd thinks he meant. To fail better, to fail gracefully and with composure, is so essential because there's no such thing as success. It's failure all the way down.

Writing itself is failure. Even the successes are failures. In the best work, the intentions of the author fall away, leaving an open field for readers to play in, and they create meanings that may have nothing to do with the author's. Jonathan Swift famously intended *Gulliver's Travels* as an indictment of all humanity but ended up leaving a story for children. The joy of language is also a torment. "Human speech is like a cracked kettle on which we tap crude rhythms for bears to dance to," Flaubert wrote, "while we long to make music that will melt the stars." Nobody knows what they're writing. Intention never aligns with result. You never know how readers will react. You never see how readers will react. It's all what quantum physicists call "spooky action at a distance." And here we come to the real crux of the matter at last: The spirit, and its daemon language, live in failure.

I am writing these words now, in a dark morning a few days before Christmas. The air has the leaden cold of Canadian winter, and I have draped myself in a blanket decorated with stitch work constellations. A strange sempiternal fog is lifting on the street. Through a fragile and nebulous and tenuous network, these words have arrived with you. Perhaps you bought them. (Thank you.) Perhaps you borrowed them. Perhaps you stole them. Perhaps a teacher forced them on you. Perhaps you're in jail. Perhaps you're in love. You might be reading them in a dorm room, or the community space of an old folks' home, or on a beach in Belize, or in the subway. Perhaps you're not reading these words at all because the publisher who commissioned them folded or refused them. I don't know. I can't know.

That discrepancy is a torment and it is a thrill, that resonance that should be impossible. The reader has that thrill, too. I know. John Keats wrote "Ode on Melancholy" for me. Specifically he wrote it for me at fifteen. He wrote it for a teenager in a suburb in a city in a country, none of which existed at the time of his writing. He may not have known it but he did. And I do not know who I am writing this for, or for what time, or to what purpose. But there is a deep longing in me—and it's not a lie, not a fraud—to make these words for you. These ephemeral connections are the substance of victory, to belong to a constellation of meanings, to alleviate a specific, minuscule cosmic loneliness. It seems like such a small satisfaction to expend your life on. It isn't. "You ask, why send my scribbles," Ovid, in his exile, asked. "Because I want to be with you somehow." Somehow, anyhow.

* * *

NO WHINING. NO complaining. Shakespeare died with unproduced plays, with manuscripts he had worked on burned to nothing, lost forever. Why should it be any different for you? This business leaves everyone, every last one, ragged.

* * *

THE GREAT INTELLECTUAL traditions begin in failure. The writers who come before writing, the figures whose words burned with such intensity that they provoked in others the beginnings of writing, were losers. The head-waters that gushed into streams that continue flowing to this day sprang from catastrophes. Socrates and Confucius and Jesus were all failures, profound failures. Their failures were the most total, the most spectacular.

* * *

SOCRATES'S LAST DAYS, if they didn't involve pointless death, would be hilarious. They read like a slapstick routine, the intellectual equivalent of a man slipping on a banana peel he himself put on the floor and falling through a manhole he himself opened. After the Athenians accused him of corrupting the young, Socrates defended himself deliberately badly, arguing that he was smarter than everybody else, and that his judges were too stupid to know how stupid they were. Once these stupid judges convicted him, they asked Socrates what punishment he believed he deserved. He told them, in so many words, to give him tenure: "If I am to suggest an appropriate penalty which is strictly in accordance with justice, I suggest free maintenance by the state." The judges sentenced him to death instead. Even then, he could easily have avoided his fate. Usually, in Athens, they killed you right after sentencing. But Socrates caught a break. The day of his trial happened to be the first day of the annual Mission to Delos, the commemoration of Theseus's victory over the Cretan minotaur, so he had a month in prison. His friends begged him to escape. He refused. He took the hemlock instead.

The story of Socrates's last days is a story of wilful pointless fiasco. The man used language to ensure his own silence. If this is what the life of a philosopher looks like, why would anyone pursue it? If wisdom cannot preserve itself, what value is wisdom? If the truth means death, why look for it?

* * *

THE FAILURE OF Confucius was less dramatic but more extensive. The greatest scholar of practical politics achieved a complete lack of influence.

After he resigned from his position as minister of crime to Duke Ding, ruler of the state of Lu, in what is now Shandong province, Confucius wandered China desperate for a job. The King of Chu considered giving him a fiefdom, but a minister advised against it. "If Confucius with such able disciples to help him were to have land of his own, that would not be to our advantage." A fair point.

Confucius even considered serving a rebel prince from the state of Jin. His disciple Zilu protested: "I heard it from you, master, that the gentleman does not enter the domain of one who in his own person does what is not good. How can you justify going there?"

Confucius answered: "Has it not been said: 'White indeed is that which can withstand black dye'? Moreover how can I allow myself to be treated like a gourd which, instead of being eaten, hangs from the end of a string?" The guy wanted to be useful. He wanted a job. Who can blame him?

Confucius did reject the offer in the end. For his virtue, he promptly began to starve. "When the provisions ran out, the followers had become so weak that none of them could rise to their feet."

Again, Zilu confronted his master: "Are there times when even gentlemen are brought to such extreme straits?" Confucius compared the virtues of a gentleman with flowers in a forest. "That no one is there to smell them does not take away their fragrance."

The wisest of all men, the best manager, couldn't even mange his own career. Confucius's life contains the futility of his message. The worldliness required to enact decency is indecent. Benevolent government isn't possible without power but power doesn't come to the benevolent.

* * *

JESUS CHRIST MAY be the most failed writer. He preached love as clearly and as evocatively as possible. In return, his friends betrayed him, his people turned against him, the authorities crucified him. After his death, his disciples gathered a bunch of his speeches into a handful of potted biographies that contradict one another and their readers used these texts primarily to justify empires. The world took to massacring his own people on the basis of what they thought he meant. Two thousand years later, Jesus has over a billion devoted fans. They get together, sometimes once a week or more, to read his stuff out loud to each other. A career could not have gone much worse or better.

* * *

SOCRATES AND CONFUCIUS and Jesus define whole traditions. They are the origins of Western philosophy, Chinese humanism, and Christianity, respectively. They're all failures. And it's not just that they're failures. They failed in ways that bring the systems of meaning they originated into question while revealing, at the same time, the absolute power of their messages. What is the life of philosophy worth if you can't convince anyone, even yourself, that you should live? What is benevolence worth if it's permanently unemployed? What is the value of love if it's betrayed and distorted at every turn? These questions aren't rhetorical. The answers become more important than the content of the works they inspired. The death of Socrates is the heart of his testimony: Philosophy must be the use of language beyond its effects, the pursuit of truth no matter the consequences. The unemployment of Confucius is the ultimate proof of his vision: Proper government will always be rare because almost nobody in power wants to follow its humbling requirements. The crucifixion of Jesus Christ has become his meaning: Love is the only answer no matter how betrayed the love. These contradictions are the substance of the traditions that followed in the wake of these men. Their failures were their triumphs. Why would it be any different for you?

* * *

A FACT THAT no one seems able to tell young writers: The quality of your writing will have very little effect on your career, and yet it is the only thing that matters. If you want to write well, the overwhelming majority of the time you will be doing so for its own sake, with a vague, not particularly sensible hope that it will somehow resonate. That's how Samuel Johnson lived. That's how George Orwell lived. That's how Ken Saro-Wiwa lived. That's how Jane Austen lived. That's how Herman Melville lived. That's how Kazi Nazrul Islam lived. That's how John Keats lived. That's how Ovid lived. That's how Li Bai and Du Fu lived. That's how Anna Akhmatova lived. That's how James Baldwin lived. Why would it be any different for you?

* * *

KNOW THIS: IF you're writing well and failing and submitting and persevering, there is no more that anyone can ask of you, even yourself.

* * *

NO WHINING. IT is a peculiar ambition to write. Most of the people you emulate died in the gutter and many, at the end, weren't worthy of the gutter. The desire to make meaning, indistinguishable from the possession of a soul, is a valid desire despite the inevitability of defeat. The loneliness of this business can be delicious, the cached privacies, the dark corners of words, verbs and their foibles, nouns and their stubbornness, the weird rhythms they take on together, the sudden gusts of sentiments, the crashes of insight. The loneliness of this business can be abyssal, holes where all you can hear is your heartbeat, your own dumb blood. There are failures right now, all over, rendering meanings, and some will be born, some will miscarry, some will be aborted, and behind them all lies that persistent urge: To be with you somehow when nobody is with you. Writers are peculiar beings with their successful failures and their failed successes. Their skins are so thin you can hold them up to the light.

* * *

IF YOU ARE not defeated in the end have you been fighting the right battle?

Epilogue: The Grand Hotel

THERE WERE OTHER hotels but this hotel was the grandest. To the boy, it was the grandest anyway. From the first time he saw it, looming towers at the centre of town, he knew he belonged inside.

His parents, passing by the Grand Hotel, would hurry him along. To them, as to most people in town, the building provoked a mixture of reverence and mockery. Nobody could remember a time when the Grand Hotel was not in dire need of repair, crumbling from rot and the ordeal of the elements. It was constantly under new management, and the new management never seemed to solve its problems. For the boy's parents, and for his aunts and uncles and cousins, and all his parents' friends, the Grand Hotel was both too good and not good enough. It was somehow both sacred and ridiculous, a holy pariah of a building. No doubt this general confusion of respect and contempt fuelled the boy's fascination.

It was a fascinating building no matter who looked at it. The facade of the Grand Hotel was a confounding mixture of the very ancient and the hypermodern—there were turrets on towers giving way to sleek all-glass walls, and farther back strange rising obelisks and what appeared to be smokestacks. The boy must have walked around the periphery several hundred times trying to make sense of it. There had to be an illusion at work, he figured, some kind of forced perspective; there was more building than seemed capable of fitting in the space. On one corner, it might look like the second level contained a Moorish courtyard, but from the other side of the corner, there seemed to be a rooftop adobe hut. If he were inside the hotel, the boy thought, he could figure it all out.

As adulthood arrived, the boy faced the same negotiations as all the other boys, the imprecations and elucidations of sex and money, but, for him, there was another question that mattered just as much: How could he get inside the Grand Hotel? The main entrance was out of the question. Burly guards in filigreed scarlet uniforms waited, with their white-gloved hands crossed, at the top of a marble staircase whose balustrades were interlocked dragons. The guards at the main entrance never had to throw anybody out because nobody ever tried to come through the main entrance. The boy chose a very small door in a very abandoned courtyard, a dirty corner filled with wintry slush, strewn with garbage, in a sub-basement off one of the parking lots. Bolstering his courage, the boy knocked. There was no reply. The boy knocked thirty more times. Sometimes he would knock and run away. Sometimes he would just stand there knocking. It made no difference.

Eventually, he began to throw himself against the door. The door budged slightly. So the boy kept throwing himself against the door. At first his shoulder hurt but then he found a rhythm. He lost track of how many times he threw himself against the door. One day it opened. A woman stood on the other side. She looked as surprised as he must have, coming out to throw some trash on the slush pile. The boy didn't need to be asked. He slipped in. He never knew if that woman came to the door because of his knocking, or by accident.

Once inside, he knew that the Grand Hotel was always where he was supposed to be. The inside was much the same as the outside, an international luxurious affair maintained shabbily. The Persian carpets were threadbare. The houseplants had been fostered to enormous heights and then abandoned. Older annexes had rotten floorboards, and the patterns on the drapes were absurdly unfashionable. Everything lay under a film of dust, but, to the boy, even the dust smelled sweet, like grass and vanilla. The people who occupied the hotel were curious: glamorous swanning pretend countesses, impish lads with filthy faces, lecturing dames with peaked noses, ancient bankrupt masters drinking themselves to death in the foyer, cliques of androgynous teenagers instructing themselves in the rites of antique orgies, patzers squabbling, a simple French girl with a parrot on her shoulder, starving Russian mothers and cheerful African schoolboys, Japanese ladies, Peruvian peasants, eunuchs and consuls, exiles and emperors. It was never clear who was a guest and who was staff. His fellow residents were strangers to one another—that much he could tell. Some seemed to have been born there. Others, like him, were eager newcomers. Still others appeared to occupy the hotel without purpose, as if they had come in to get out of the rain.

The boy realized that the door he had entered was only the beginning. The hotel was all doors, door after door after door. It was exciting and deflating at the same time: So much to go into. He wanted to see it all.

The boy began throwing himself against the doors of various rooms. He selected the doors closest to him at first, then, having overheard some of the conversations of the other residents, he began to pick the doors that appeared to have the longest hallways behind them. It was like some enormous game or puzzle, and while there was no competition, he couldn't help comparing himself to how others did. Others could enter doors that he could not enter. He could enter some doors others couldn't. Some would approach a door and it seemed to open as if by a gust of wind. Others struggled with the keys that should have worked but didn't. Was it the people or was it the doors? There were some rooms that only people who had been in before were allowed to enter. Entrance into other rooms was selected by lottery. Yet other doors were open only to members of certain races or nations. Still other doors opened at random.

The boy knew himself. He was ultimately a brute. All he could figure out how to do was to throw himself against doors. His shoulder hurt, but doors eventually opened. He told himself that the doors opened because of his work. The truth was that he could determine only a faint connection between his efforts and whether that door opened. Sometimes he might throw himself against a door for several months, and then a much larger door across the room would open by itself. He wondered, at times, if more doors would open if he stopped throwing himself against them. If he could manage stillness, maybe those on the other side would be welcoming. Unfortunately, it was not in his nature to be still. The fact that a door was closed to him was enough that he had to see it open. And once a door opened, he forgot it had ever been closed. Maybe the answer to the point of opening the doors was on the other side. He was sure that if he had not thrown himself against the doors, even the doors that had not opened, then no doors would have opened. If the hotel was a puzzle, it was a stupid one. You had to throw yourself against the door even though it might have no connection to that door opening.

As time passed, as the boy became a man and the man aged, he remembered the first times he'd seen the Grand Hotel. He had been inside for so long that it took effort to recreate how the edifice must look from the outside. His parents, and his family, and all their friends and everyone he knew, had been wrong. It was neither a sacred nor a pariah place. It was just a bunch of rooms, with doors, inhabited mainly by drunks and charlatans who were quite ordinary. The horror and the glory were the same: There were always more rooms, always other doors. The longing to enter one room, once satisfied, generated more longings to enter more rooms. The multiplication of hunger felt, to the man, like a pusher's trap, a sleight of hand played on his brain chemistry. Had he been fooled? But for what? By whom? If he was being scammed, what was the scam? This Grand Hotel—what was it? A labyrinth? A prison machine? Some kind of turbine powered by the movement of the residents? Who owned it? How was it built?

The man counted his blessings. He was, after all, in a beautiful hotel and dry. His parents had been right. He was both not good enough for the Grand Hotel, and too good for it. Its existence was a statement that the world was worth the cost of its significance.

His doubts were only pauses, rests for his shoulder. He needed a plan. No plan made sense. No plan could make sense. He made a plan. Looking through all the rooms he had been through, which were not few, he picked out the biggest door he could find, the heaviest, and he threw himself against it, and he threw himself against it, and he threw himself against it.

A Note on How I Work

I TEND TO explore my feelings and thoughts in essays and articles for various publications before I put them down in a book. The text you're holding in your hands, for example, derived from three essays: A piece I wrote for the *New York Times* in 2014, "Failure Is Our Muse"; a 2015 post for *Esquire* about David Foster Wallace's suicide; and bits from an essay called "The Obama Years," in the *Los Angeles Review of Books* in 2016. I just took a few bits, though, and they're pretty chopped up.

Bibliography

Ayscough, Florence. *Tu Fu: The Autobiography of a Chinese Poet*. Vols 1–2. Boston: Houghton Mifflin, 1929.

Bate, W. Jackson. *Samuel Johnson: A Biography*. New York: Harcourt Brace Jovanovich, 1977.

Boethius. *The Consolation of Philosophy*. Trans. Peter Walsh. Oxford: Oxford University Press, 2008.

Bowker, Gordon. *James Joyce: A New Biography*. New York: Farrar, Straus and Giroux, 2013.

Boyd, Brian. *Vladimir Nabokov*, vols 1 and 2. Princeton: Princeton University Press, 1993.

Bruccoli, Matthew. *Fitzgerald and Hemingway: A Dangerous Friendship*. New York: Carroll & Graf, 1994

Caplan, Usher. *Like One That Dreamed: A Portrait of A. M. Klein*. Toronto: McGraw Hill Ryerson, 1982.

Chin, Annping. *The Authentic Confucius: A Life of Thought and Politics*. New York: Simon and Schuster, 2007.

Claassen, Jo-Marie. *Displaced Persons: The Literature of Exile from Cicero to Boethius*. London: University of Wisconsin Press, 1999.

Donaldson, Scott. *Fitzgerald & Hemingway: Works and Days*. New York: Columbia University Press, 2009.

Ferdowsi, Abolqasem. *Shahnameh: The Persian Book of Kings*. New York: Penguin Classics, 2016.

Frank, Joseph. *Dostoevsky: A Writer in His Time*. Princeton: Princeton University Press, 2012.

Hawkes, David. *John Milton: A Hero of Our Time*. New York: Counterpoint, 2011.

Jamison, Kay Redfield. *Touched with Fire: Manic-Depressive Illness and the Artistic Temperament*. New York: Free Press, 1996.

Johnson, Samuel. *The Major Works*. Oxford: Oxford University Press, 2009.

Keene, Donald. *Five Modern Japanese Novelists*. New York: Columbia University Press, 2005.

Leeming, David. *James Baldwin: A Biography*. New York: Arcade, 2015.

Lyons, Phyllis I. *The Saga of Dazai Osamu: A Critical Study with Translations*. Stanford: Stanford University Press, 1985.

Ovid. *Sorrows of an Exile*. Trans. A. D. Melville, with an introduction and notes by E. J. Kenney. Oxford: Clarendon Press, 1992.

Parker, Hershel. *Herman Melville: A Biography*, vols 1 and 2. Baltimore: Johns Hopkins University Press, 2005.

Plato. *The Last Days of Socrates*. Trans. Hugh Tredennick, with an introduction by Harold Tarrant. London: Penguin Classics, 2003.

Rilke, Rainer Maria. *Letters to a Young Poet*. Trans. Stephen Mitchell. New York: Modern Library, 2010.

Robertson-Lorant, Laurie. *Melville: A Biography*. New York: Clarkson Potter, 1996.

Roe, Nicholas. *John Keats: A New Life*. New Haven: Yale University Press, 2013.

Schuman, Michael. *Confucius and the World He Created.* New York: Basic Books, 2015.

Sima Qian. *Records of the Grand Historian: Qin Dynasty.* New York: Columbia University Press, 1996.

Swift, Daniel. *The Bughouse: The Poetry, Politics, and Madness of Ezra Pound.* New York: Farrar, Straus and Giroux, 2017.

Ueda, Makoto. *Modern Japanese Writers and the Nature of Literature.* Stanford: Stanford University Press, 1976.

Unger, Miles J. *Machiavelli: A Biography.* New York: Simon and Schuster, 2012.

Waley, Arthur. *The Poetry and Career of Li Po: 701–762 A.D.* New York: Macmillan, 1950.

STEPHEN MARCHE is a novelist, essayist and cultural commentator. He is the author of half a dozen books, and has written opinion pieces and essays for the *New Yorker*, the *New York Times*, *The Atlantic*, *Esquire*, *The Walrus* and many others. He lives in Toronto with his wife and children.

Other titles in the **FIELD NOTES** series

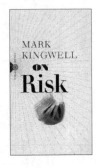

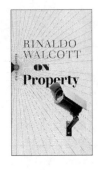

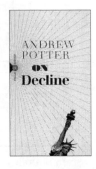

FIELD (#1) NOTES

MARK KINGWELL

ON RISK

FIELD (#2) NOTES

RINALDO WALCOTT

ON PROPERTY

FIELD (#3) NOTES

ANDREW POTTER

ON DECLINE

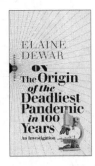

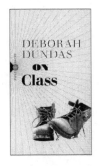

FIELD (#4) NOTES

ELAINE DEWAR

ON THE ORIGIN OF

THE DEADLIEST

PANDEMIC

IN 100 YEARS

FIELD (#5) NOTES

JASON GURIEL

ON BROWSING

FIELD (#7) NOTES

DEBORAH DUNDAS

ON CLASS